to

_____

from

_____

For Daisy, Elliot and Tom, with love A.A.

Text by Lois Rock
Illustrations copyright © 2006 Alex Ayliffe
This edition copyright © 2006 Lion Hudson

The moral rights of the author and illustrator
have been asserted

A Lion Children's Book
an imprint of
Lion Hudson plc
Mayfield House, 256 Banbury Road,
Oxford OX2 7DH, England
www.lionhudson.com
ISBN-13: 978 0 7459 4919 2
ISBN-10: 0 7459 4919 3

First edition 2006
1 3 5 7 9 10 8 6 4 2 0

A catalogue record for this book is available
from the British Library

Typeset in 22/30 Baskerville BT
Printed and bound in China

my very first
Christmas

Words by
Lois Rock

Pictures by
Alex Ayliffe

LION
CHILDREN'S

Contents

The Baby in the Manger

The flowers bobbed and curtsied as the angel Gabriel passed by.

"Nazareth looks lovely in the spring," said Gabriel, "but I have work to do. I need to give Mary a message from God.

"I can see her over there."

Mary was startled to see the angel.

"Don't be afraid," said Gabriel. "God has chosen you to be the mother of a very special baby—Jesus."

The news puzzled Mary.

"I can't be a mother," she answered.
"I'm not Joseph's wife yet."

"The baby will be God's son," replied
Gabriel. "Everything will happen because
of God."

"Oh," said Mary.
"I will always
do what God
wants."

Joseph soon heard the news about Mary.

"She's going to have a baby—but it's not mine," he wept.

"I really want to marry her—but is that still the right thing to do?"

In a dream, an angel spoke to him.

"Of course you must marry Mary. God has chosen you to look after her and the baby."

Joseph woke up feeling happy again.

Then more news arrived—news for everyone.

"The emperor has made a new law," said the messenger. "All of you must go to your home towns and put your names on a big list."

"Why?" asked the people of Nazareth.

"It's to check you're all paying your tax money," said the messenger glumly.

Joseph went to speak to Mary.

"You must come with me to Bethlehem," he said. "We shall be on the list as husband and wife."

Joseph and Mary plodded down the long road to Bethlehem.

Because of the emperor's new law, lots of people were going to their home towns.

When Mary and Joseph reached Bethlehem, there was no room left in the inn.

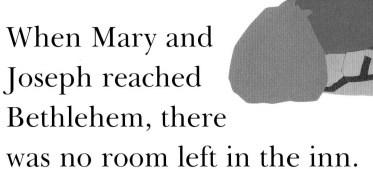

"My baby is going to be born very soon," whispered Mary. "We need somewhere to stay for the night."

At last, they found shelter in a stable.

"It's not a proper room," said Joseph, "but it's all we have. I hope the animals don't bother you."

There, in the stable, Mary's baby was born.

She wrapped him in swaddling clothes to keep him snug and warm.

"This feeding trough is a bit like a cradle," said Joseph. "I can make it snug for the baby."

"It's perfect," said Mary, as she laid baby
Jesus in the manger.

Shepherds and Angels

It was night-time in Bethlehem. Out on the hillside, shepherds were guarding their sheep.

"We need to keep them safe from foxes," said one.

"And jackals," said another.

"And wolves and bears and lions," said the little shepherd boy. "I'm not afraid of anything."

Suddenly a light flashed through the sky, brighter than lightning.

The shepherds hugged each other in fright.

The shepherd boy hid behind a sheep.

Then they saw the angel.

"Don't be afraid," said
the angel. "I have
good news. Tonight,
in Bethlehem, God's
son has been born.

"He will be greater than
the greatest king.

"He will bring joy to all the world.

"Tonight, in Bethlehem, he is cradled
in a manger."

All at once, it seemed as if the stars
in the sky started to dance.

In their glittering light, a choir
of angels sang joyful songs.

"Glory to God
in heaven!"

"Peace to everyone
on earth!"

The shepherds gazed in wonder.

When the songs were sung, the night was once again still and silent.

"Let's go to Bethlehem," whispered the shepherd boy. "I want to know if the message is true…or if I've just been dreaming."

Off they all went to the little town on the hilltop.

Everywhere, they listened hard. They were hoping to hear the gentle cry of a newborn baby.

At last they found the place. Joseph and Mary and baby Jesus were there.

The little shepherd boy suddenly felt shy. Mary smiled. "Come closer," she said.

He tiptoed nearer and touched the baby's hand.

"Now tell me everything about the angels," she said. "I want to know exactly what they said."

When the telling was done, the
shepherds set off, back to the hillside.

Mary held her baby as she watched
them step out into the dark night.

The shepherd boy turned back
to wave.

It seemed, for a moment,
as if he were looking
right into heaven.

He felt that he would never
be afraid ever again.

Wise Men and a Star

The men looked up at the night sky. The star shone back at them, clear and bright.

"I think it is a messenger star," said one.

"I think I understand the message," said the second. "A new king has been born."

"Then we should go and look for him," said the third.

They all agreed that this was the wise thing to do.

They set off on their journey. The star lit
their way.

There were hills and valleys, mile after mile.

At last they came to the city of Jerusalem.
The royal palace there was very grand.

"We are looking for a newborn king,"
they told the townspeople. "Is he here?"

Inside the palace, King Herod was puzzled.

"Can anyone explain what's going on?"
he growled.

The priests came with their precious books.

"Listen to what's written here: God will
send a special king one day. He will be
born in Bethlehem."

Herod sent for the wise men.

"Try to find the king in Bethlehem," he said.
"I, too, want to see him."

He watched the men go, then muttered,
"I want to get rid of this king."

The wise men went along the road
to Bethlehem.

The star lit the way.

It hung low over a little house in the
town.

Inside, the wise men found Mary and
her little boy, Jesus.

The men bowed to show their respect.

"I bring a gift of gold," said one, "for the king who will be rich beyond all telling."

"I bring frankincense," said the second.

"Like a priest, this king will help people be friends with God."

"I bring myrrh," said the third. "It is ointment that heals. This king will be able to heal everyone and everything."

After the gift-giving, the men whispered together, "Let's not go back to Herod. It feels wrong to tell him about this wonderful king."

They went home by a different road.

In a dream, an angel spoke to Joseph.

"Hurry. Take Mary and Jesus far away from here. Keep them safe, so Jesus can grow up and truly become God's special king."

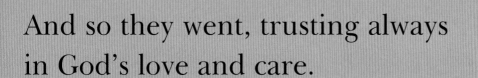

And so they went, trusting always
in God's love and care.

The Tree of Bethlehem

High in a cedar tree, a little owl ruffled her feathers.

"Ooh-hoo," she said, as she peered out on the hilltop. "I feel a co-old wind.

"Don't blo-ow the sno-ow to Bethlehem," she warned the wind.

But the cold wind blew on, leaving a carpet of snow.

In among the thorn bushes, the sheep huddled closely together.

"Baa-ad weather is coming," they bleated.

The ewes snuggled closer to their lambs.

"Don't blow the snow to Bee-ethlehem," they warned the wind.

But the cold wind blew on, leaving icicles on every twig.

The wind blew down to the stream
and set the willow branches swaying.

"Eek, it's icy," squeaked the mice.
They rubbed their paws together.

One brave mouse spoke aloud.

"Keep the sleet out of Bethlehem," he said.

But the cold wind blew on, scattering hailstones in the water.

Just outside Bethlehem stood a grove of olive trees.

A white dove sheltered under the leaves.

"Oooooh," cooed the dove. "Tooo coool, tooo coool."

The leaves began to whisper to the wind. "Shh, shh, a baby is sleeping. Shh."

"Where," said the wind, "where, where?"

It rattled a door and woke some children.

"What's going on?" they said. They got up and followed the wind.

The cold wind didn't seem to care. It blew on, whistling into every nook and cranny.

It reached a stable in Bethlehem. Outside stood a little fir tree.

The wind tried to creep around to the
doorway, but the fir tree would not let it
in. The tree stood tall, pointing to heaven.

The cold wind blew up to the sky.

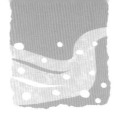

Just then a woman came to the stable door, holding a tiny baby.

All at once, twelve goldfinches appeared on the fir tree, singing merrily.

Then the wind blew down from the sky. It was warm now and it brought a trail of stars.

High above, the angels sang.

By the tree, the children laughed for joy.

The Fourth Wise Man

The wise men looked up at the sky. "Look at that star!" they said. "It is a sign. A new king has been born."

"We must go and worship him," they agreed, "and take him gifts."

As they set out, one wise man placed a glittering box in his travel bag.

"I am going to give the king gold," he said.

Two of his companions nodded wisely, but the fourth wise man looked glum.

"I don't have a gift yet," he said.

The four wise men went on their way.
The star shone above them.

The fourth wise man was worried. When
they stopped, he asked the second wise man,
"Do you have a gift?"

"Yes," he said. "I chose frankincense."

"It burns with the sweetest smell—a smell that helps people think about God."

"Oh," said the fourth wise man.

"The new king will help people say prayers to God," said his friend.

For many nights the wise men rode along dusty roads. The fourth wise man got a blister from holding the reins of his camel.

"Never mind," said the third wise man. "I have ointment made with myrrh to soothe the pain."

"Thank you," said the fourth wise man.

"I have more," said the third wise man. "See—I have pure myrrh for the king. I believe he will be a great healer."

The fourth wise man sighed. "I'd almost decided on myrrh," he said. "Now I'm too late."

The star pointed the way to Bethlehem.
It shone on a little house. Inside were a
mother and her baby boy.

The three wise men went to give their gifts.

"I've nothing to give," said the fourth wise man to himself. "I might as well give some water to the camels."

He leaned over the well. The star in the sky was mirrored in the water.

He let down the bucket.

When he pulled it up again, the star was in his bucket.

It twinkled like jewels.

"It's perfect," said the fourth wise man.
"The baby would love to see it."

Without really thinking, he rushed
into the house.

It must have been a miracle. The star
went on shining in the bucket.

"It's shining like a little piece of heaven,"
said the mother. "It's a perfect gift."

Suddenly everyone knew that the little
baby must be the king
of heaven.

Little Brigid

Little Brigid sat by the fire.
She was mending
her cloak.

"Oh dear," she sighed.
"There seem to be
holes everywhere.
The cloth is old.

"Really, I should make a new cloak.
Winter has only just begun. But I'm
so busy every day."

She was tired, too. She rubbed her
eyes and went to bed.

Brigid always got up early to do the daily jobs. First she mixed a bowl of bread and left it to rise.

Then she went to call the cows for milking.

Then she came back to the kitchen.

She baked the bread.

She made a pot of soup and
left it cooking.

She churned some butter.

One winter's day, she heard
a knock at the door.

Outside was a poor man. "Can you spare something to eat?" he begged.

"Yes," said Brigid. "Come inside."

She gave him warm soup and fresh bread spread with new butter.

Later, as she waved him goodbye, she saw a young woman with a crutch.

"Come and rest," called Brigid. "You must let your ankle get better."

She took off the grubby bandage and washed the woman's feet.

She wrapped the hurt ankle in a new bandage. "It feels better already," said the woman.

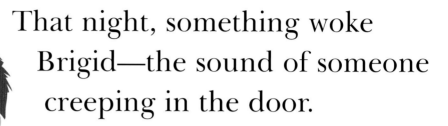

That night, something woke Brigid—the sound of someone creeping in the door.

"Please help," said a shy voice.

"You poor child," said Brigid. "You're wearing just a nightshirt."

"Please come and rock the baby to sleep," said the little child. "His mother is so tired."

"Yes, of course," said Brigid, wrapping her cloak around her.

"You show me the way."

The little child seemed almost to fly along the woodland path. Brigid could hardly keep up.

All at once, they were there. Brigid
found herself in a tumbledown room.
At one end were a donkey and an ox.
Nearer the door were a mother
and her baby.

"Oh, he's only just been born!"
said Brigid to the mother.
"Let me wrap him in
my cloak. I will rock
him to sleep and
you can rest."

Softly she sang a lullaby. The little child joined in the tune. He had the voice of an angel.

As the sun rose, the mother awoke. "Bless you for coming to help," she said.

Brigid hurried away. She felt warm
and snug.

"My cloak!" she said. "It's better
than when it was new!"

The cloth was thick and soft. The holes had gone. In their place were stars stitched in threads of gold.

Baboushka

"I've got the fire going," said Baboushka to herself. "That's a good start to a busy day."

Next she made a big pot of soup and left it to cook.

Then she began to sweep.

She heard a knock on
the door.

"Bother! Who can that
be?" she said. "I'm still
very busy."

Outside there were three men. She did not know who they were.

But she did notice their warm coats, made from the very best sort of cloth. They must be rich!

"We are cold," said the men. "May we warm ourselves by your fire?"

"If you take your boots off," said Baboushka. "I'm halfway through cleaning."

The snow from their boots left puddles by the door. Baboushka tutted.

"May we have some food?" they asked. "We can pay," they said.

Baboushka served them bread and soup. She wanted to be kind… but there was so much to do.

She felt pleased when the men said it was time to go.

"We are looking for a newborn baby king," said one. "He will be the king of heaven and earth," said the second.

"We have gifts to give him," said
the third. "Would you like to come
with us?"

"No, thank you," said Baboushka.
"I can't leave the house in a mess.
Later, maybe."

Baboushka cleaned all day. She scrubbed and she polished.

"Housework!" she said. "There's always something to be done. I'll begin again tomorrow."

She woke up in the middle of the night. A bright star was shining outside her window. And what was that music?

She could hear angels singing.

"Oh dear," she said to herself. "It is a song for the newborn king. I must take the child a gift. It can't be very far."

The next day she went and bought toys—a whole basketful of them.

She walked and she walked, looking for the king.

Outside one house, she heard a little
child laughing. She tiptoed inside.

"Is he here?" she asked. There was
no answer. "I shall leave a toy anyway.
The king would like that," she said.

The same thing happened
again and again.

To this day, no one has seen Baboushka, but people say she is still looking for the king. In every house where she hears a little child laughing, she still leaves a gift.

"The king would like that," she
says...and then she travels on.

Good King Wenceslas

The little page boy snuggled into bed. It had been the happiest Christmas ever.

In the room next door, his master, King Wenceslas, closed the shutters. "The feast went well," he said. "Everyone seemed happy. I shall sleep well."

Soon he fell asleep.

In the night, the shutters blew open.
Moonlight shone in through the window.

"Brrr," said the king.
"I shall have to go
and close the shutters
again."

He went to
the window.

He saw someone outside in the
snow—a man picking up twigs.
He had a big bundle of them.

"Who is he?" the king wondered.
"He looks very poor. I wonder if
my page boy knows him?"

He called his page boy,
and the two stood
at the window.
They watched
the man trudge
away.

"He has a long
walk home,
and all uphill,"
said the page boy.

"Well," said the king, "we must follow him
and give him gifts."

They both got dressed in their
warmest clothes.

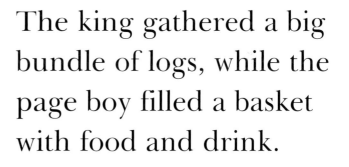

The king gathered a big
bundle of logs, while the
page boy filled a basket
with food and drink.

Outside, all was dark. Snow clouds
hid the moon. The wind blew harder
than ever.

The page boy's
basket felt very
heavy.

Then he tumbled in the snow.

"I'm fine," he said bravely. "It's just that my feet are very cold."

"Walk in my footsteps," said the king. "It will be easier for you."

As he did, the snow seemed less deep. "My feet are warm now," the page boy announced.

He looked down. Then he bent to look more closely.

A miracle had happened!

The king's steps had made a path through the snow, and spring flowers had begun to bloom.

The king and his page boy brought their gifts to the poor man's house. The logs made the fire burn bright and warm. The food was the kind everyone liked best, and together they had a feast.

It was like Christmas Day all over again.

The happiest Christmas ever.

The Little Juggler

Pietro learned to juggle
when he was a little boy.

As he grew taller,
he learned to
juggle better
and better.

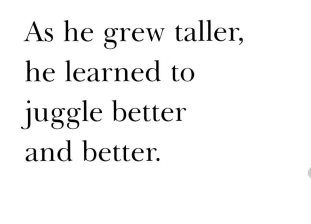

People clapped and cheered.

Then he grew old. He did not juggle well anymore.

Sometimes he dropped things.

People laughed and jeered.

Pietro sighed. "I shall have to stop juggling," he said to himself. "I shall become a monk and spend my time doing whatever pleases God."

He joined a monastery. The old monk in charge welcomed him.

Some of the other monks were cross.

"Pietro sings out of tune," whispered one grumpily.

"His voice will spoil our carol singing," muttered another.

"I know!" said a third. "He's new. We'll make him clean the church for Christmas. Then he won't have time for singing."

Alone in the church, Pietro said a prayer
as he swept and polished. "I know I'm
not a good monk," he said. "But
I still want to thank you, God,
for all you have given me."

In front of him was a
statue—a statue of Mary
and the baby Jesus.

Suddenly, he ran and fetched
a bag. Inside were seven
juggling balls.

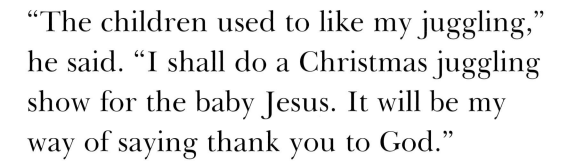

"The children used to like my juggling,"
he said. "I shall do a Christmas juggling
show for the baby Jesus. It will be my
way of saying thank you to God."

He began carefully, with three
juggling balls…then five…then
all seven.

"Thank you for all my happy
years of juggling!" he called out.

Behind him a door creaked open.
The monks had come to rehearse
their carols. They all gasped.

"Stop at once!" ordered
the grumpy monk.

Pietro hurried to pick up his juggling
balls. He found six.

The seventh was out of reach. It was in the hand of the baby Jesus.

"God has heard your special thank-you prayer," said the old monk in charge.

Everyone clapped and cheered.

The Baker's Christmas

It was Christmas Eve. The baker was making bread.

He heard a knock at the window.

"It's carol-singing time," called the children.

114

"I'm too busy," said the baker.

He shaped the dough into loaves
and put them by the oven.

He poked the fire to make it burn
bright and hot.

When he looked up, he couldn't believe what he saw.

Every single loaf of dough had turned into the shape of a child.

One by one, they jumped down to the floor.

Right before his eyes, they grew to full size.
Then they all ran out the door.

"Come back!" cried the
baker, as he rushed out
after them.

The dough children laughed and tumbled in the snow.

They ran to the village square. There, they hid among the real boys and girls.

Everyone had gathered around the little scene of Mary and Joseph and baby Jesus in the manger.

They all began to sing carols. The baker couldn't help but join in.

They sang and sang until the first star shone.

Then, in the sunset sky, the baker saw something.

There were angels, brighter than any flame. They were kneading the clouds as if they were lumps of dough and shaping them into loaves.

All at once the baker remembered.

"Dear me," he said. "My baking!"

He looked for the dough children,
but there were none to be seen.

He hurried back to
his kitchen.

The fire was glowing nicely.

The loaves were just as he had first made them—except that they had risen, round and plump, just as they should.

"I must have been dreaming about the dough children," he said, as he put the loaves into the oven.

"But now I have time to make gingerbread boys and gingerbread girls for Christmas— I can make all kinds of things!"

On Christmas morning, when people
came to buy their bread, he had
wonderful gifts for everyone.

125

Christmas Words

angels   messengers from heaven who sang when Jesus was born

Bethlehem   the town where Jesus was born

carols   happy Christmas songs

Christmas   birthday celebrations for Jesus; his royal title is Christ

fir tree   a decorated fir tree makes the world cheerful and bright at Christmas

gifts wise men brought gifts to Jesus; people give each other gifts at Christmas

Jesus the Christmas baby, cradled in a manger

Mary Jesus' mother

shepherds angels told shepherds that Jesus had been born

star a bright star led the wise men to Bethlehem